This copy of

THE GARDEN OF LOVE

comes to

JOHN AND PAULINE

A.K.A NANNA AND DADDAD !

with love from

ROMANI, SARAH, ISAIAH,

SOL x.

THE GARDEN OF LOVE

Copyright © 1995 by Eagle

Published by Crossway Books
a division of Good News Publishers
1300 Crescent Street
Wheaton, Illinois 60187

First British edition published by Eagle, 1995

First U.S. edition published by Crossway Books, 1998

First U.S. printing, 1998

Printed in Singapore

Scripture taken from the HOLY BIBLE: NEW INTERNATIONAL VERSION®.
Copyright © 1973, 1978, 1984 by International Bible Society. Used by
permission of Zondervan Publishing House. All rights reserved.

The "NIV" and "New International Version" trademarks are registered in the
United States Patent and Trademark Office by International Bible Society. Use of
either trademark requires the permission of International Bible Society.

LIBRARY OF CONGRESS CATALOGING-IN-PUBLICATION DATA
Bible. English. New International. Selections. 1998.
    The garden of love : God's love revealed. — 1st U.S. ed.
        p.   cm.
    Includes bibliographical references.
    1. God—Love—Biblical teaching.   2. God—Love—Prayer-books and
devotions—English.   I. Crossway Books.   II. Title.
BS544.B47 1998   220.5'20816—dc21   97-38453
ISBN 0-89107-991-2

08   07   06   05   04   03   02   01   00   99   98
15   14   13   12   11   10   9   8   7   6   5   4   3   2   1

THE GARDEN OF LOVE

God's Love Revealed

CROSSWAY BOOKS

I HAVE LOVED YOU WITH AN EVERLASTING LOVE

❧

I have loved you with an everlasting love;

I have drawn you with loving-kindness.

I will build you up again and

you will be rebuilt.

JEREMIAH 31:3-4

A Yorkshire View
Edmund John Niemann

THE LORD YOUR GOD
IS WITH YOU

❧

The Lord your God is with you,

he is mighty to save.

He will take great delight in you,

he will quiet you with his love,

he will rejoice over you with singing.

ZEPHANIAH 3:17

Mother and Child
Charles James Lewis

FOR GOD SO LOVED THE WORLD

❧

For God so loved the world
that he gave his one and only Son,
that whoever believes in him
shall not perish but have eternal life.

JOHN 3:16

But God demonstrates
his own love for us in this:
While we were still sinners,
Christ died for us.

ROMANS 5:8

———————

L'Immensité
Gustave Courbet

PRAISE THE LORD!

Praise the LORD, O my soul;
all my inmost being, praise his holy name.
Praise the LORD, O my soul,
and forget not all his benefits.
He forgives all my sins
and heals all my diseases.
He redeems my life from the pit
and crowns me with love and compassion.
He satisfies my desire with good things,
so that my youth is renewed like the eagle's . . .

The LORD is compassionate and gracious,
slow to anger, abounding in love.

PSALM 103:1-5, 8

Loch Lomond
David Farquharson

LET US LOVE ONE ANOTHER

Dear friends, let us love one another, for love comes from God. Everyone who loves has been born of God and knows God. Whoever does not love does not know God, because God is love. This is how God showed his love among us: He sent his one and only Son into the world that we might live through him. This is love: not that we loved God, but that he loved us and sent his Son as an atoning sacrifice for our sins. Dear friends, since God so loved us, we also ought to love one another. No one has ever seen God; but if we love each other, God lives in us and his love is made complete in us.

I JOHN 4:7-12

Ring-a-Ring-of-Roses-Oh!
Frederick Morgan

HOW DEEP IS THE LOVE OF CHRIST

And I pray that you, being rooted and established in love, may have power, together with all the saints, to grasp how wide and long and high and deep is the love of Christ, and to know this love that surpasses knowledge—that you may be filled to the measure of all the fullness of God.

EPHESIANS 3:17-19

For I am convinced that neither death nor life, neither angels nor demons, neither the present nor the future, nor any powers, neither height nor depth, nor anything else in all creation, will be able to separate us from the love of God that is in Christ Jesus our Lord.

ROMANS 8:38-39

The Coniston Valley, The Lake District
William Lakin Turner

THE KINDNESS OF THE LORD

❧

I will tell of the kindnesses of the LORD, the deeds for which he is to be praised, according to all the LORD has done for us—yes, the many good things he has done for the house of Israel, according to his compassion and many kindnesses. He said, "Surely they are my people, sons who will not be false to me"; and so he became their Savior. In all their distress he too was distressed, and the angel of his presence saved them. In his love and mercy he redeemed them; he lifted them up and carried them all the days of old.

ISAIAH 63:7-9

The Primrose Woods
Elizabeth Stanhope Forbes

MY LOVE WILL
NEVER BE SHAKEN

❧

"Though the mountains be shaken

and the hills be removed,

yet my unfailing love for you will not be shaken

nor my covenant of peace be removed,"

says the Lord who has compassion on you.

ISAIAH 54:10

Tig Bridge
Helen Allingham

HE WHO LOVES ME

"Whoever has my commands and obeys them,
he is the one who loves me. He who loves me will be
loved by my Father, and I too will love him
and show myself to him."

"If anyone loves me, he will obey my teaching.
My Father will love him, and we will come to him
and make our home with him."

JOHN 14:21, 23

A Devonshire Mill Stream
Robert J. Hammond

GIVE THANKS TO THE LORD

Give thanks to the LORD, for he is good.
His love endures forever.
Give thanks to the God of gods.
His love endures forever.
Give thanks to the Lord of lords:
His love endures forever.
To him who alone does great wonders,
His love endures forever.
who by his understanding made the heavens,
His love endures forever.
who spread out the earth upon the waters,
His love endures forever.
who made the great lights—
His love endures forever.
the sun to govern the day,
His love endures forever.
the moon and stars to govern the night;
His love endures forever.
Give thanks to the God of heaven.
His love endures forever.

PSALM 136:1-9, 26

At the Foot of the Trossachs
Alfred de Breanski

I WILL NOT FORGET YOU

❧

Cast all your anxiety on him
because he cares for you.

I PETER 5:7

"Can a mother forget the baby at her breast
and have no compassion on the child she has borne?
Though she may forget, I will not forget you!
See, I have engraved you on the palms of my hands."

ISAIAH 49:15-16

Maternal Care
Evert Pieters

TRUST IN GOD

❧

"Do not let your hearts be troubled. Trust in God; trust also in me. In my Father's house are many rooms; if it were not so, I would have told you. I am going there to prepare a place for you. And if I go and prepare a place for you, I will come back and take you to be with me that you also may be where I am."

JOHN 14:1-3

"My sheep listen to my voice; I know them, and they follow me. I give them eternal life, and they shall never perish; no one can snatch them out of my hand. My Father, who has given them to me, is greater than all; no one can snatch them out of my Father's hand. I and the Father are one."

JOHN 10:27-30

Children and Sheep in Spring
Luigi Chialiva

I WILL HEAL YOU

❧

"I will heal their waywardness and love them freely, for my anger has turned away from them. I will be like the dew to Israel; he will blossom like a lily. Like a cedar of Lebanon he will send down his roots; his young shoots will grow. His splendor will be like an olive tree, his fragrance like a cedar of Lebanon. Men will dwell again in his shade. He will flourish like the corn. He will blossom like a vine, and his fame will be like the wine from Lebanon."

HOSEA 14:4-7

Harvesting
Helen Allingham

WHATEVER YOU DO,
DO IT FOR THE LORD

❧

*Whatever you do, work at it with all your heart,
as working for the Lord, not for men, since you know
that you will receive an inheritance from
the Lord as a reward. It is the Lord
Christ you are serving.*

COLOSSIANS 3:23-24

The Mowers
Sir George Clausen

PHOTOGRAPHIC CREDITS

Crossway Books is grateful to the copyright holders listed below, and to The Bridgeman Art Library and The Fine Art Photographic Library in particular for their kind permission to reproduce the paintings selected to complement the text.

COVER   *Mother and Child*, by Charles James Lewis, 1830-92, Christopher Wood Gallery, London (Bridgeman).

1.   *A Yorkshire View*, by Edmund John Niemann, 1813-76, (Fine Art).

2.   *Mother and Child*, by Charles James Lewis, 1830-92, Christopher Wood Gallery, London (Bridgeman).

3.   *L'Immensité*, by Gustave Courbet, 1819-77, Victoria & Albert Museum (Bridgeman).

4.   *Loch Lomond*, by David Farquharson, 1840-1907 (Fine Art).

5.   *Ring-a-Ring-of-Roses-Oh!*, by Frederick Morgan, 1856-1927, Townley Hall Art Gallery & Museum, Burnely (Bridgeman).

6.   *The Coniston Valley, The Lake District*, by William Lakin Turner, 1867-1936, courtesy of Colemore Galleries, Henley-In Arden (Fine Art).

7.   *The Primrose Woods*, by Elizabeth Stanhope Forbes, 1859-1912, Whitford & Hughes, London (Bridgeman).

8.   *Tig Bridge*, by Helen Allingham, 1848-1926 (Eagle).

9.   *A Devonshire Mill Stream*, by Robert J. Hammond, c. 1900? (Fine Art).

10.   *At the Foot of the Trossachs*, by Alfred de Breanski, 1852-1928 (Fine Art).

11.   *Maternal Care*, by Evert Pieters, 1856-1932, Josef Mensing Gallery, Hamm-Ryhnern (Bridgeman).

12.   *Children and Sheep in Spring*, by Luigi Chialiva, c. 1900 Gavin Graham Gallery, London (Bridgeman).

13.   *Harvesting*, by Helen Allingham, 1848-1926 (Eagle).

14.   *The Mowers*, by Sir George Clausen, 1852-1944, Usher Gallery, Lincoln (Bridgeman).